Come Alive

A 30-DAY DEVOTIONAL JOURNEY OF HOPE AND RENEWAL

OUTRE/CH®

Come Alive: A 30-Day Devotional Journey of Hope and Renewal
© 2018 by Outreach, Inc.

Published by Outreach, Inc., Colorado Springs, CO 80919
www.Outreach.com

Unless otherwise noted, Scripture quotations in this publication are taken from THE HOLY BIBLE, NEW INTERNATIONAL VERSION®, NIV® Copyright © 1973, 1978, 1984, 2011 by Biblica, Inc.® Used by permission. All rights reserved worldwide. Also used is the NEW AMERICAN STANDARD BIBLE® (NASB), Copyright © 1960,1962,1963,1968,1971,1972,1973,1975,1977,1995 by The Lockman Foundation. Used by permission.

ISBN: 9781635107159
Cover Design by Tim Downs
Interior Design by Alexia Garaventa
Written by Jeremy Jones
Program Manager: Erica Chumbley

Printed in the United States of America

CONTENTS

INTRODUCTION

More than two thousand years ago, God's plan of redemption altered the world forever. The power of sin and death was broken through the crucifixion and resurrection of Jesus Christ that first Easter. Death was defeated. True life, spiritual life, God's life triumphed. And today we continue to come alive to God's story of love as our lives and our world are transformed by His grace.

That is reason to celebrate. It is reason to respond to God's open arms and His invitation to draw near to Him. This book is a devotional journey through the events of Holy Week and beyond. The lessons, Scripture, and reflection or small-group questions are all here to guide you through a life-giving experience of the truth of Easter and of God's power to transform you into a new creation. You can use these short daily readings and questions on your own or in a group setting. Follow them flexibly to fit your schedule and needs. Most important, let them draw you into an encounter with God and His invitation to come alive in the truest sense possible.

ACTIVITY IDEAS

There are so many fun ways to celebrate the Easter season and create meaningful experiences with friends, family, classes, and small groups. Here are some activity ideas to ignite your creativity throughout Holy Week and beyond. The tangible examples may be especially valuable for helping children grasp the powerful truth expressed in Easter. But we all can use a fresh reminder or hands-on encounter of God at work in our world. Enjoy the chance to be creative and come alive to God's truth in a new way.

PASSOVER

Host a traditional Passover meal. Set up cushions on the floor, and have someone wash the feet of guests as they arrive. You may choose to research, make, and serve traditional Seder foods or simply serve a favorite meal. Talk about the history of the Passover meal (from Exodus 12) and about how it foreshadowed Jesus's sacrifice on the cross.

BUILD YOUR OWN CROSS

Using 2-by-4 wood pieces, build a cross. Older kids will enjoy the process of measuring, cutting, and nailing or tying the wood together. Decide where the cross will be displayed to determine the size. Leave the cross up during Holy Week as a reminder of Jesus's sacrifice. Family or group members may want to write prayers of thanks or confession on papers and nail them to the cross throughout the week. You may choose to drape purple fabric around the cross or create a crown of thorns to hang from it as a reminder that Jesus the King died for you.

EASTER EGG STORY

Retell the story of the resurrection with children by creating "resurrection eggs." In six plastic eggs of different colors, place the following (one per egg): a bread crumb, a paper cross, a strip of cloth, a rock, and a piece of candy. One egg will remain empty. As you tell the story of Jesus's resurrection, allow kids to open each egg and discuss its meaning:

1. **Bread crumb:** Jesus ate dinner with His friends. (Luke 22:14–15)

2. **Cross:** The next day, Jesus died on the cross. (John 19:17–18)

3. **Strip of cloth:** He was wrapped in cloth and placed in a tomb. (John 19:40)

4. **Rock:** A huge stone was placed in front of the tomb. (Matthew 27:59–60)

5. **Empty egg:** Jesus's friends came to the tomb and saw the stone had been moved. The tomb was empty! (Luke 24:1–3)

6. **Candy:** We celebrate because Jesus is alive! (Matthew 28:5–6)

EASTER HIKE OR WALK

Take a hike or walk, and talk about how nature reflects the new life Christ offers us. You may see the new growth of spring, such as butterflies, flowers, or water. Reflect on how nature praises God and demonstrates His creativity and imagination.

DELIVERY BASKETS

Create baskets to deliver to community members in need—at a shelter, through an adoption organization, at a nursing home, or through some other local organization. (As a time-saving alternative, you might purchase Easter lilies to deliver instead.) When you deliver the baskets, spend time talking with and listening to people in your community you may not have met before.

PASSION PLAY

Plan to attend a local passion play. Can't find one? Put together a performance of your own. Don't worry about making it extravagant. Just like Christmas pageants can tell the story of Christmas, a simple play about Easter can bring to life the events of Holy Week and the celebration of new life we receive in Christ.

EASTER SNACKS

Make some fun Easter snacks to share with friends, neighbors, or group members.

- Join pretzel sticks together in the shape of a cross, securing them with a dab of frosting.

- Make pancakes, and have a contest for who can create the best pancake shape. You might try a cross, a stone tomb, a palm branch, or any other Easter shapes you can come up with.

- Bake classic Rice Krispies Treats, but shape them into crosses.

EMPTY TOMB ROLLS

These rolls are a fun, simple baking activity with a great lesson. Spread out the dough from canned refrigerated crescent rolls. Take a white marshmallow and explain that Jesus was perfect, without sin. Then dip the marshmallow in melted butter and explain that when Jesus died, His friends anointed His body with oils. Next dip the marshmallow in a mixture of sugar and cinnamon and explain that it represents the spices they also used to anoint the body of Christ before burying Him in a tomb. Next put each marshmallow on a strip of crescent roll dough and roll it up, making sure to pinch all sides closed. Explain that this represents the strips of cloth they used to wrap Jesus's body. Finally, brush the tops of the rolls with a little bit of butter, and bake according to the instructions on the crescent roll package. Talk about how Jesus was in the tomb for three days. When the rolls are finished, take them out and allow them to cool slightly. Then open one carefully—surprise! Jesus is no longer in the tomb. The marshmallow is gone, giving a tasty example that Jesus has risen. Enjoy your rolls as you read John 20:1–18 together.

NEW LIFE SHIRTS

Buy two white T-shirts for each person in your family or group and lots of fabric paint. Let each person design their own shirt—it can be as simple or as wild and crazy as they like. Then talk about how now that they've colored the shirts, there is no way to make them white again. Even the best bleach in the world would not remove the stain of the paint. Then hold up a new white shirt and explain that the only way to have a white shirt again is to receive a new one. Talk about how the same is true with our lives—stained by sin, we must receive a new life and become a new creation through Jesus.

CONTAINER GARDEN TOMB

Create a container garden that represents where Jesus was buried. Fill the base of a large planter with soil. Bury a small flowerpot under the soil at an angle so the open mouth is facing up and out, like a cave. Then place a large landscape stone just to the side of the open tomb (flowerpot). Add three stick crosses to the back of the garden, some small pebbles, and any other details you would like to see. Talk about how when the women came to the tomb on Easter Sunday, they were met by the stone that was rolled away and two angels who announced that Jesus was alive!

Holy Week

 PALM SUNDAY   **GOOD FRIDAY**   **EASTER SUNDAY**

1

COME ALIVE
TO GOD'S STORY
(PALM SUNDAY)

For God so loved the world that he gave his one and only Son, that whoever believes in him shall not perish but have eternal life. For God did not send his Son into the world to condemn the world, but to save the world through him.

—John 3:16–17

As palm branches waved and songs and shouts of praise resounded, Jesus entered Jerusalem that first Palm Sunday. Matthew described the scene like this: "The crowds that went ahead of him and those that followed shouted, 'Hosanna to the Son of David!' 'Blessed is he who comes in the name of the Lord!' 'Hosanna in the highest heaven!'" (Matthew 21:9).

Can you imagine what must have been going through the mind of Jesus? He heard the praise of the crowds yet knew all along the pain, suffering, and sacrifice that lay ahead.

The ride into Jerusalem was the next step of His journey to fulfill God's bigger story that began at the creation of the world. Jesus's coming and His sacrifice were not afterthoughts in God's plan. This wasn't a fix for a glitch in the system. This was God's ultimate story of redemption. The Old Testament is filled with smaller stories of redemption that serve as foreshadowing of the ultimate work: Noah and the flood, Abraham and Isaac, the Passover lamb in the exodus from Egypt, to name a few. But as Jesus entered Jerusalem, He marked the beginning of a week that by God's design would change the world forever.

The palm branches we wave represent victory—the ultimate victory of God's love that saved the world, the ultimate victory that changes our lives.

God, I join in shouting "Hosanna!" today. Thank You that You have had a plan from the beginning to save and restore me. Please open my heart this week as I journey through and come alive to Your story of redemption. Amen.

How do you imagine it might have felt to be in the crowd in Jerusalem when Jesus rode in on Palm Sunday?

How does knowing the end of the story of Jesus's sacrifice change how we view this day?

What Old Testament stories do you recall that mirror the redemptive story of Jesus's coming?

What can you do this week to dig deeper into Jesus's journey to the cross?

2

COME ALIVE
TO GOD'S LOVE

For I am convinced that neither death nor life, neither an-gels nor demons, neither the present nor the future, nor any powers, neither height nor depth, nor anything else in all creation, will be able to separate us from the love of God that is in Christ Jesus our Lord.

—Romans 8:38–39

As we walk toward Easter, we are surrounded by so much cultural packaging. Easter eggs and dresses and bright colors and springs flowers and baby bunnies. And chocolate. Don't forget the chocolate. And it's all good and fun. But the truth of this Holy Week is that we have a lot of darkness to walk through before we get to the celebration—maybe it's in our past; maybe we're facing it right now. In the midst of our pain and suffering, we can hold to the hope and truth of a greater love. A love that nothing can separate us from.

Singer-songwriter David Wilcox captured a beautiful word picture in his song "Show the Way." He compared finding hope and a reason to believe with a play written to show something stronger than hate. *Wouldn't it look like evil will win? Wouldn't it look like the hero arrives too late?* he asked. But Wilcox suggested there was something greater at work all along, even building the stage from its very beginning:

> *There is evil cast around us*
>
> *But it's love that wrote the play*
>
> *For in this darkness love can show the way.*

It is God, in His great love, who wrote the script for Easter—and for our lives. Through the confusion and pain that occurred in the original Easter week and the confusion and pain that occur in our lives, God's love shows the way. Because of that, because we know nothing in the world can separate us from His love, we continue to journey toward the cross—and the resurrection.

God, thank You that Your great and perfect love underlies the Easter story and is knit into the fabric of the universe. Help me to rest in the truth that nothing can separate me from Your inexhaustible love. Amen.

How does it feel to know that God's love was the source of such great sacrifice?

Are there times you feel separated from God's love? What can serve as your reminder of the promise in today's verses from Romans?

Describe a time when you felt overwhelmed by God's love.

How will you respond to God's love?

3

COME ALIVE
TO THE LIGHT

When Jesus spoke again to the people, he said, "I am the light of the world. Whoever follows me will never walk in darkness, but will have the light of life."

—John 8:12

The world Jesus entered was not so unlike our world today. There was war and greed and violence and evil. So when He told His followers that He was the light of the world, they understood. They lived in dark times, and their world needed the light.

The Gospel of John begins with the imagery of light: "In him was life, and that life was the light of all mankind. The light shines in the darkness, and the darkness has not overcome it" (John 1:4–5). But it doesn't always feel that way, does it? Sometimes it can seem like darkness has the upper hand. But have you ever sat in darkness and looked for light? It doesn't take much. Just a faint flicker of a flame, a distant glimmer of a star, and the darkness is no longer complete.

When we follow Jesus, we always have Him with us as the light of life. No matter what darkness permeates your life, no matter how hard things get, look for the Light. The darkness cannot overcome it.

God, this world sometimes feels so dark, and I can have a hard time seeing the light. Please draw near to me in those times. Fill me with Your life and Your light. Thank You that You are the Light of the World so I never walk in darkness. Amen.

Describe a time when darkness felt overwhelming in your life.

How did you get through? What was your source of light?

What can you do to look for and focus on the Light?

How can you be a light, a reflector or bearer of Jesus's light, to others?

4

COME ALIVE
TO FAITH

*Now faith is confidence in what we hope for and assurance
about what we do not see.*

—Hebrews 11:1

We depend on sight for so many things. Even though people tell us we can't always believe what we see, it is one of our primary senses, and we tend to rely on it for proof of what is going on in the world around us, especially for important life-changing events. And while we have the Bible to tell us about historic events like Holy Week, we weren't there. We aren't eyewitnesses.

That makes faith tough. It doesn't follow the rules of vision. Yet God calls us to believe what we cannot see. He calls us to faith—confidence and assurance in what we can't see. We have to trust the word of others, our experience of His faithfulness, and the confirmation we receive when we step out in action. It's a choice we have to make every day to push back against the natural world and engage the spiritual world. It's a practice to make 2 Corinthians 5:7 our reality: "For we live by faith, not by sight."

God, it is so hard to release my natural instincts and to walk by faith. Please give me confidence and assurance in You as I step toward You again and again in faith. Amen.

Have you ever had to do something without being able to see? What was the experience like?

When have you stepped out in faith and experienced the assurance of God's leading and presence?

How can the shared experiences of others help you to live by faith?

Is there an area of life where you need to let go of the need to see, and embrace faith? How will you take a step toward doing that?

5

COME ALIVE
TO SERVICE

*This is how we know what love is: Jesus Christ laid down
his life for us. And we ought to lay down our lives
for our brothers and sisters.*

—1 John 3:16

Dirt roads. Sandals. Hot sun. It's a recipe for really stinky
feet! Which is why servants often washed the feet of guests
when they arrived at someone's home during Jesus's day.
But as Jesus's disciples gathered to celebrate the traditional Passover supper together in Jerusalem, it was Jesus who
did the foot washing. He wrapped a towel around Himself, knelt in front of each disciple, and washed and dried
their cracked and calloused feet.

It was the ultimate act of service. Knowing what lay
before Him, Jesus set an example for His followers, and for
us, of humility and love. Just days earlier He was hailed
as king as He rode into town. And the day after He would

suffer and die by crucifixion. But on this day He knelt and served those He cared most about. In so many ways He showed us love by laying down His life for us.

Jesus, thank You for Your example of humility and love. Thank You that in the midst of the painful and consuming events of Holy Week, You didn't demand attention but instead served others in love. Please help me to follow Your example and lay down my life for my brothers and sisters. Amen.

Have you ever had your feet washed? How would you describe the experience?

What acts of service would be equivalent to this in today's society?

What makes it hard for you to serve others? What obstacles keep you from it?

How can you decide to serve others in your community this week?

6

COME ALIVE TO SACRIFICE (GOOD FRIDAY)

*God presented Christ as a sacrifice of atonement, through
the shedding of his blood—to be received by faith.*

—Romans 3:25

Why do we call it good? On the surface, this Friday is the worst day in all of history: the Son of God betrayed, crucified, and dead. We can only see the beauty in today because we know what happens on Sunday. But to skip ahead misses the power of Good Friday. To simply look beyond the cross to the empty tomb minimizes the incredible sacrifice Jesus made.

Instead, we must linger here for a moment. We must look up into the eyes of love, look into the face of the Son of God willingly dying to save us from our sin. To look at the cross forces us to reset our lives according to His sacrifice.

Because of His death, we are given life. As the apostle Peter reminded us, "'He himself bore our sins' in his body on the cross, so that we might die to sins and live for righteousness; 'by his wounds you have been healed'" (1 Peter 2:24). When we take the time to hold Christ's suffering in our hearts, it creates overwhelming gratitude and humility.

Jesus, Your sacrifice is my salvation. Help me to grasp the magnitude of what You did for me and for the world—and to live out of gratitude for it. Thank You. Amen.

Why is it difficult to spend time focused on the sacrifice Jesus made?

Why do you think it is important to do so? What effect has it had on your heart?

What feelings are stirred up when you ponder the pain and suffering Jesus went through?

How can a deeper understanding of Jesus's sacrifice impact your relationship with Him and with others?

7

COME ALIVE
TO FORGIVENESS

*If we confess our sins, he is faithful
and just and will forgive us our sins and purify
us from all unrighteousness.*

—*1 John 1:9*

Have you ever written on a whiteboard in a classroom or at a meeting? When you're done, you erase the board . . . but if you look closely, you can still see traces of what was written. We wipe it clean, but the residue still lingers. Do you ever think of forgiveness that way? We know God takes away our sin, but we still feel like it can be seen. We suspect it's still there, just less obvious. But when we treat forgiveness that way, we mock the sacrifice of Jesus.

The forgiveness God offers is complete. He purifies us from all unrighteousness. Colossians 2:13 says we were dead in sin but have been made alive in Christ. There is no halfway between dead and alive. Paul clarified: "He forgave us all our sins, having canceled the charge of our legal indebtedness, which stood against us and condemned us; he has taken it away, nailing it to the cross" (Colossians 2:13–14). Our sin is gone. In fact, Jeremiah 31:34 says God doesn't even remember it: "For I will forgive their wickedness and will remember their sins no more." Forgiveness in Jesus is not a faded, half-erased whiteboard. He has cleansed you and cleared your record. He has washed away your shame, leaving you white as snow.

God, thank You that You don't offer partial forgiveness. Help me to live in the truth that my sins are erased, gone, canceled, nailed to the cross forever. Amen.

Have you asked for and accepted God's forgiveness through Jesus?

Do you still feel like there are sins in your life that have not been erased? Why are they still holding on?

What is the difference between forgiveness of sin and the natural consequences of sin that may still remain?

How can the knowledge that you are forgiven change the way you live and the choices you make?

8

COME ALIVE TO NEW LIFE (EASTER SUNDAY)

Therefore, if anyone is in Christ, the new creation has come: The old has gone, the new is here!

—2 Corinthians 5:17

"He is risen! He is risen, indeed! Hallelujah!" The joyful cries of God's people on Easter echo around the world. The waiting is over, and the tomb is empty. Jesus is alive! And not only is *He* alive, He brings new life to those who believe.

We are newly created because of Jesus's resurrection. And most important, the way is open for us to be one with Him. We are not just saved; we are invited into the family of God. John wrote, "Yet to all who did receive him, to those who believed in his name, he gave the right to become children of God" (John 1:12). God wants to bring you into His family and give you a new title: accepted, forgiven, loved child of God. His welcome is wide open. Will you join Him?

God, I rejoice in the new life You bring through Your Son, Jesus. Thank You that You turned darkness into light and brought forgiveness through Your love. Help me to live as a new creation and as Your loved child. Amen.

What imagery comes to mind when you think of new creations? How do those apply to the new creation you are in Christ?

How does it feel to be a child of God? How does it impact your sense of identity?

What will you do today to celebrate that Jesus is alive?

How can you carry the joy of Easter forward into your daily life this week?

Coming alive beyond Easter

9

COME ALIVE
TO BELIEF

Immediately the boy's father exclaimed, "I do believe;
help me overcome my unbelief!"

—*Mark 9:24*

Doubt can feel like a closed door. It seems to be a roadblock that keeps us from believing. It's natural to consider doubt as the opposite of belief or faith. But in our relationship to God, that proves not to be the case. In fact, doubt is sometimes the very proof that our faith is sincere and growing. By questioning and admitting our doubt, we actually open the door for God to help our faith grow deeper.

In the Gospel of Mark, a father brings his son to Jesus to be healed. He believes Jesus can heal the boy but is naturally worried and unsure of whether this life-changing event could actually happen. So when Jesus responds to the father's request by saying, "Everything is possible for one who believes" (verse 23), the father's honest and passionate response is "I do believe; help me overcome my unbelief!" (verse 24). But Jesus did not scold the man or send him away for his disbelief. He healed his son.

We are human. We are imperfect. And so the two—belief and disbelief—go hand in hand. Even famous believers like C. S. Lewis and Mother Teresa struggled. But when we turn to Jesus in honesty and ask for His help, our disbelief is met with the enduring power and faithfulness of God's grace and love, allowing us to come more alive to belief.

God, I run to You in faith like the father in the Bible story, but I carry with me doubts and questions. Thank You that my own weakness doesn't impact Your strength. Thank You that You never change, that You welcome me with open arms, and that You honor my belief even when I struggle. I believe; please help my unbelief today. Amen.

What do you struggle to believe?

When do you feel this most intensely?

How could allowing yourself to admit your doubt help you work through it?

Who do you trust enough to talk with about your beliefs and doubts?

10

COME ALIVE
TO GRACE

But because of his great love for us, God,
who is rich in mercy, made us alive with Christ
even when we were dead in transgressions—it is
by grace you have been saved.

—Ephesians 2:4–5

An acrostic simple enough for children to understand sums up the complexity of grace.

God's
Riches
At
Christ's
Expense

It puts into five words the incredible event that occurred when Jesus defeated death on the cross and cleared the way for us to experience forgiveness and freedom from sin. God's love and mercy are free to us. Undeserved. Life-changing. Grace is the greatest gift ever given, and when we come alive to grace through Christ, we are truly alive.

So once we receive this gift of grace, how do we live in response? We allow grace to permeate every aspect of our lives. Grace becomes the guide for how we speak to others (Colossians 4:6) and how we serve others (1 Peter 4:10). It establishes our identity (Colossians 2:9–10), our strength (Hebrews 13:9), and so much more. God's free gift keeps giving as He pours into our lives and transforms us to be more like Him.

God, I do not deserve Your mercy and love, but thank You that You have given me these gifts. Your grace is amazing! Please help me learn to live according to the riches You've given through grace and help me to extend that grace to those around me. Amen.

Have you experienced God's grace in your life? How?

What happens when you go from death to life through grace?

How does receiving such an undeserved gift make you feel?

What does it look like to extend that grace to other people?

11

COME ALIVE
TO TRUST

*Trust in the LORD with all your heart and lean not on
your own understanding; in all your ways submit to him,
and he will make your paths straight.*

—Proverbs 3:5–6

Have you ever been lost? Taken a wrong turn? Ended up
somewhere with no idea of the right way to head? What
did you do? Maybe you've been lost in the wilderness with
no cell coverage, left to trust a map and compass to get
you on the right path. Or in today's world of technology,
maybe you've simply turned to the smartphone or GPS
at your fingertips. We trust them to guide us into and
out of places we've never been before. Why do we trust
these things? Because they've proven time and again to
be accurate and to give us the information we need to get
where we need to go.

The same can be true for trusting in God. The more we turn to Him, the more He proves to us that He will guide us. We see that His way is the best way. But in life, sometimes we are like that person who is convinced they can find the way without the help of a map or directions. Instead of trusting the proven source, they rely on themselves. When we come alive to trust, we lay aside our pride and our stubborn confidence in order to follow the One who made the map and who can direct us in the way we should go.

God, thank You that You know the twists and turns of my life even better than I do. Please help me to trust You with all my heart and to follow Your way. Amen.

Is there an area of your life where you are questioning which way to go?

Do you trust that leaning on God is better than leaning on your own understanding?

What makes it difficult for you to trust?

Can you recall times when you trusted God and His way and it proved to be best?

12

COME ALIVE
TO HOPE

But those who hope in the LORD *will renew their strength.*
They will soar on wings like eagles; they will run and not
grow weary, they will walk and not be faint.

—Isaiah 40:31

The best dreams are flying dreams. Have you ever had one? Where you can fly, soaring effortlessly above the ground, catching the wind in your wings, and floating on air? Life is hard work, and we often find ourselves tired, weak, and exhausted by the demands that meet us every day. So the concept of soaring, of running without growing tired appeals to us at a very real level.

It's exactly that imagery that Isaiah used to describe what happens when we put our hope in the Lord. Our strength is renewed. We can run and walk without growing weary. We can soar. Why? Because God's hope takes us beyond our current circumstances and allows us to see the long view. He gives us strength for today because our future with Him is secure. Coming alive to hope doesn't remove us from life's challenges, but it does keep our focus on something so much greater. And it renews our strength to run toward it.

Lord, my hope is in You. Help me to actively focus on that hope and allow You to renew my strength. Help me to experience the promise that I will soar and run even in the midst of the challenges I face today. Amen.

Where do you feel like your hope is today?

What is the focus of your energy and time?

How might coming alive to hope strengthen you in the midst of your current circumstances?

When have you experienced the renewing of your strength through hope?

13

COME ALIVE
TO REST

Come to me, all you who are weary and burdened, and I will give you rest. Take my yoke upon you and learn from me, for I am gentle and humble in heart, and you will find rest for your souls. For my yoke is easy and my burden is light.

—*Matthew 11:28–30*

Study after study confirms what we all know each time the alarm clock goes off—we all need more rest. As a society, we are working ourselves into the ground and destroying our bodies, minds, and souls. So why is it so hard for us to rest? Somehow the demands of our lives, schedules, school, jobs, and relationships all squeeze out room for rest.

But to all of us who are frazzled and exhausted, who have reached the end of our ropes, Jesus calls. He calls us to set aside time with Him—not as another thing on the to-do list but as an opportunity for rest. And it doesn't have to look like a scheduled meeting in the conference room of life. A long walk, a bike ride, casting the fishing rod, drawing, painting, or a simple cup of tea by the fire can help bring us to Jesus if we'll turn our attention toward Him. And when we come to Him, He promises rest for our souls. When we lay our lives, our struggles, our fears and hurts in His hands, He gives us rest in return.

God, I am tired. And I find it hard to see how I can stop and rest with so many things demanding my attention and time. Please help me to come to You and receive Your rest for my soul. Amen.

On a scale of 1 to 10, rate your current need for rest.

How are sleep and rest different? How might they work hand in hand?

Can you name two schedule changes to your day that could help create room for rest?

Describe a time when you felt alive to God's rest in your life.

14

COME ALIVE
TO PEACE

Do not be anxious about anything, but in every situation, by prayer and petition, with thanksgiving, present your requests to God. And the peace of God, which transcends all understanding, will guard your hearts and your minds in Christ Jesus.

—Philippians 4:6–7

When you think of peace, do you think of it as an absence of things? An absence of noise, violence, trouble, conflict? The dictionary does define peace as freedom from these things. But coming alive to God's peace is so much more than an absence; it is His presence with us. Jesus is the Prince of Peace. And He offers us His peace, which defies our human understanding.

God's peace comes in the midst of noise, violence, trouble, and conflict. His peace guards our hearts and minds when we face those things in our lives. It is why Peter told us to "cast all your anxiety on him because he cares for you" (1 Peter 5:7). It's an instruction, but it's also a promise—not that trouble or anxiety will disappear, but that He cares for us and will fill us with His peace that transcends our trouble.

God, when I feel anxious, please help me to come to You in prayer and to cast all my anxiety on You. Thank You that You promise a peace that I can't even understand but that guards my heart and mind through the presence of Jesus in my life. Amen.

Describe a time when you experienced God's peace.

How does the process of talking with God about your worries and fears transform you?

What is troubling you now?

What can you do today to experience God's presence?

15

COME ALIVE
TO COURAGE

Joshua said to them, "Do not be afraid; do not be discouraged. Be strong and courageous."

—Joshua 10:25

There is no courage without fear. Think about that. If we were never afraid of anything, it wouldn't require courage to overcome it. Courage is strength in the face of fear, pain, and grief. It is not the absence of these things, but action in the midst of them.

Yet so often we are overcome by our fear. We let fear weaken us and prevent us from taking action. When Jesus was about to leave His disciples, He knew they were afraid and would face many situations that would bring more fear, pain, and grief. So He challenged them to have courage—not because they were strong enough to overcome, but because He had already overcome. He told them, "I have told you these things, so that in me you may have peace. In this world you will have trouble. But take heart! I have overcome the world" (John 16:33).

As believers, we can find courage in the fact that Jesus has already won the battle. While we will face fear in our lives, we know the ultimate end of the story, and this can spur us on to action in the face of fear. He has overcome, so we can too.

God, when I am afraid, please give me courage. Help me to take action and to find courage and peace in the knowledge that You have overcome the world. Instead of allowing fear to control my life, please fill me with Your strength and courage to truly live. Amen.

Describe a time when you felt fear but acted with courage.

Think of someone you consider courageous. What do you admire about the way that person lives?

What fear is controlling your life right now?

How can you surrender that fear to God and come alive to courage?

16

COME ALIVE
TO PRAYER

Let us then approach God's throne of grace with confidence, so that we may receive mercy and find grace to help us in our time of need.

—Hebrews 4:16

In the celebration of Easter, we rightly focus on the death and resurrection of Jesus, which brings us forgiveness and true life. But in that process, something else happened as well. Matthew 27 tells us that at the moment Jesus died, the curtain in the temple was torn from top to bottom. This curtain separated the Holy of Holies from the rest of the temple where people were allowed to go. The curtain represented the separation between a holy God and sinful people. But when Jesus died, it was torn in two. Jesus not only brought us forgiveness, He cleared the way for us to be one with God again. So we can go to God directly, speak to Him directly, and relate with Him directly.

This understanding changes prayer from a duty we are to perform into an amazing privilege to be in conversation with the God of the universe. Prayer is about communicating with God and allowing our dialogue with Him to shape and change our attitudes, our outlook, our spirit, and the very nature of our being. This is new life.

God, thank You that You made a way for me to know You. Thank You that I can approach Your throne of grace with confidence, knowing that You desire relationship. Let's talk, and as we do, please reshape my viewpoint of prayer, of life, of You. Please draw me into Your heart. Amen.

When you think of prayer, what do you picture?

How could seeing it in a new light change the way you approach prayer and your relationship with God?

What prayers have you seen answered in your life? What prayers do you feel are unanswered?

What would you most like to change about the way you talk with God?

17

COME ALIVE
TO PURPOSE

He has shown you, O mortal, what is good. And what does the LORD *require of you? To act justly and to love mercy and to walk humbly with your God.*

—Micah 6:8

Where should I go to school? What job should I take? Who should I marry? What friendships should I pursue? Where should I live? We all want answers to the big questions of life. And while God cares about the details of our lives (after all, He's numbered the hairs on our heads!), He also cares more about our purpose than our positions in life. And He has given us a clear vision of purpose in Micah 6:8.

All of our decisions and actions should be measured by the overall guidance of what the Lord requires: to act justly, to love mercy, and to walk humbly with God. This is God's standard and expectation. It can look different for different people in different places in life, but it acts as a and informs our decisions. ...se and pour our energy into ...her life decisions come into

...wers to questions about ...y life and what decisions ...ou that You've given this ...e help me to discover ways that I can better come alive to Your purpose. Let the details of my life follow and support Your bigger designs and purpose. Amen.

Do you feel like your life reflects this purpose? In what ways?

What are some practical ways that God's overall purpose for your life can impact your daily decisions?

What is one way you'd like to act justly, love mercy, or walk humbly?

How can we as a family, group, community, or church better fulfill this purpose with each other and the people we know?

18

COME ALIVE
TO PRIORITIES

*"Love the Lord your God with all your heart and with
all your soul and with all your mind and with all your
strength." The second is this: "Love your neighbor as yourself." There is no commandment greater than these.*

—*Mark 12:30–31*

Gary Keller cofounded one of the largest real estate compa-
nies in the world. And he often speaks to the importance of
priorities through his concept of "one thing." By knowing
their one thing, people are able to prioritize and make better decisions. Today's verse from Mark could be considered
God's "one thing" for us. It's what we are to prioritize above
all else—to love God with all our heart, soul, mind, and
strength. That one thing informs everything we do, including the second thing, which is to love others.

Do you find it hard to make decisions or to figure out
how to spend your time? Looking at every decision and

every circumstance through the lens of how it helps you better love God with all of your heart will keep pulling you back to what is most important in life. When you love God and love others, all else is secondary.

God, thank You for Your amazing love. Please forgive me for my distraction and ingratitude. Draw me into Your love as I turn to You, and let that love consume me, fill me, and overflow from me as my "one thing" today. Amen.

If someone looked at your life from the outside, what would they guess is your "one thing" based on the way you prioritize your time, energy, and money?

How can loving God first help you prioritize the other things in your life?

What would be most difficult for you to move lower on the priority list?

How does loving God naturally flow into loving others? Where is it a struggle for you?

19

COME ALIVE
TO RELATIONSHIPS

Dear friends, since God so loved us, we also ought to love one another. No one has ever seen God; but if we love one another, God lives in us and his love is made complete in us.

—1 John 4:11–12

Today's verses, as well as Philippians 2:1–11, paint a picture of how we should imitate the humility of Christ in our relationships with others. We are to do nothing out of selfish ambition, but constantly look to put the interests of others above our own.

That can be hard to do even with the people we get along with, so what about relationships that are difficult? What about people you dislike or disagree with? Perhaps the first step in loving them is to learn more, to consider them worthy of our time and energy. At the moment when you'd like to walk away or ignore someone, lean into the relationship and love that person first through listening.

Ask the people in your life meaningful questions, and keep digging to learn more. As we listen and understand and serve others, God's love is made complete in us—we love others just as God first loved us.

> *God, help me to truly love those around me. It's not easy, and there are relationships I'd rather ignore. But just as I received Your love, I want to share that love with others. Please give me courage, strength, and understanding so that my love may be sincere. Thank You that You first loved me. Amen.*

Who needs you to listen and to love in humility in order to restore a relationship in your life?

What is the biggest challenge in that relationship? Why is it hard to love?

What questions can you ask in order to better understand this person?

Who might you invite into the relationship in order to help the conversations be most meaningful?

20

COME ALIVE
TO FINANCES

For where your treasure is, there your heart will be also.
—Matthew 6:21

Do you believe this? Do you believe that your treasure is a reflection of your heart? Jesus made it clear that our treasure and our hope for the future are to be placed in God alone. Does that mean we should give everything away and live on the streets? No. But it does mean many of us need to examine our desires and actions and be sure Christ is at the center of our lives—including our bank accounts.

While there are many places in the Bible that speak to saving, giving, debt, and the traps of money, 1 Timothy provides some clear and practical instructions for all of us in regard to our finances: "Instruct those who are rich in this present world not to be conceited or to fix their hope on the uncertainty of riches, but on God, who richly supplies us with all things to enjoy. Instruct them to do good, to be rich in good works, to be generous and ready to share, storing up for themselves the treasure of a good foundation for the future, so that they may take hold of that which is life indeed" (1 Timothy 6:17–19, NASB). No matter how much or how little money we have, our hope is to be in God rather than riches. Living with an open hand, receiving from God, and giving generously to others are the best ways to come alive in the area of finances. An open hand when it comes to money leaves us free to grab hold of true abundant life in Jesus.

God, thank You for the many ways You have blessed me. Please help me to see everything I have as belonging to You. Help me to live generously, with an open hand, ready to give and receive freely as I trust in You. Amen.

Do you consider yourself to be rich? Why or why not? How does your financial wealth compare with that of the majority of the world?

Based on your actions and choices related to money, where would others say your treasure is? Where do you say your treasure is?

What makes it difficult for you to trust God with your finances?

Name one area where you would like to be more generous and open-handed with your finances.

21

COME ALIVE TO WAITING

Wait for the LORD; be strong and take heart and wait for the LORD.

—Psalm 27:14

Who likes waiting? Nobody! Our whole culture (and most product marketing plans) is built around reducing the amount of time we spend waiting for anything. Microwave ovens, high-speed Internet, next-day delivery—it's all about getting things we want faster. In fact, when we have to wait, we often feel frustration and anxiety! We aren't very good at waiting. In fact, we may even see it as a complete waste of time.

But God's time is not the same as ours, and the Bible is full of stories of waiting. The people of Israel waited thousands of years for the Messiah. Mary and Martha waited days for Jesus to come heal their brother, Lazarus—so long, in fact, that their brother died! Moses waited years and still never got to enter the Promised Land. So what is God's purpose in making us wait? Bottom line is that He is more concerned with an internal result than an external one. Waiting builds patience, character, and a deeper dependence on God. It's why the psalmist encouraged us to be strong, take heart, and wait for the Lord. Waiting produces good things in us— even when we don't like it.

God, thank You that You care much more about the depth of my character than the speed of my life. Please help me to stay strong as I wait on You, trusting that the work You are doing in my heart is worth the wait. Amen.

What is your most common reaction to waiting in everyday situations? Frustration? Anger? Depression? Anxiety?

Is it harder or easier for you to wait on the really important things in life?

How can understanding God's purpose in His slower timetable help you stay strong as you wait for Him?

What can you do to grow deeper in your faith and make the time meaningful when you feel like you are waiting on God for something in your life?

22

COME ALIVE
TO PRAISE

I will exalt you, my God the King; I will praise your name for ever and ever. Every day I will praise you and extol your name for ever and ever.

—Psalm 145:1–2

Traditional or contemporary? Active or still? In a group or alone? There are so many debates about *how* we praise God that sometimes we forget to address the more important *why*. Why do we praise God? Does He need our praise? Do we need it?

There are many things we receive when we praise God. The activity changes our perspective. It teaches us about the character of God. It helps us to become more like Him. But at the core of why we praise is the fact that God simply inspires praise. When we realize who He is and what He has done, the natural response is to say, "Wow!" In fact, the Bible says that all of creation, the entire universe, praises God. "Praise the LORD. Praise the LORD from the heavens; praise him in the heights above. Praise him, all his angels; praise him, all his heavenly hosts. Praise him, sun and moon; praise him, all you shining stars. Praise him, you highest heavens and you waters above the skies . . . you great sea creatures and all ocean depths, lightning and hail, snow and clouds, stormy winds that do his bidding, you mountains and all hills, fruit trees and all cedars, wild animals and all cattle, small creatures and flying birds, kings of the earth and all nations, you princes and all rulers on earth, young men and women, old men and children" (Psalm 148:1–4, 7–12).

And when Jesus's opponents told Him to silence the people praising Him as He entered Jerusalem for Holy Week, His response was that if they were quiet, even the rocks would cry out (Luke 19:40)! So why do we praise God? Praise cannot be stopped. When we turn our focus to Him, God's greatness, His goodness, His love, His power all inspire us and the whole earth to respond with wonder, exultation, humility, and expression—praise.

God, I praise You today for who You are. I praise You because You are worthy. Please purify my heart and allow my responses and reactions to be pleasing to You today. Amen.

What motivates you to praise God?

What is your most natural way to express praise and worship to God?

How can you praise God through your every-day activities? What changes them from simple actions to acts of praise?

Is it important to praise God with other people? Why or why not?

23

COME ALIVE
TO WEAKNESS

But he said to me, "My grace is sufficient for you, for my power is made perfect in weakness." Therefore I will boast all the more gladly about my weaknesses, so that Christ's power may rest on me. That is why, for Christ's sake, I delight in weaknesses, in insults, in hardships, in persecutions, in difficulties. For when I am weak, then I am strong.

—*2 Corinthians 12:9–10*

Have you ever noticed that living as a follower of Christ means living in an opposite world? Really! The last are first. Death brings life. Obedience is freedom. Coming alive to weakness belongs in this same category of opposites. It doesn't follow our natural thinking, but the Bible is clear that when we are weak, we are actually at our strongest. Why? Because it is in our weakness that we recognize and rely more heavily on God and allow His power to take control. God's grace and strength are so much greater than any weakness in us!

While none of us naturally strives to be weak, we can live with it in a different way as we take a lesson from Paul, who said he delighted in, and even boasted about, his weakness. When we recognize our own limitations, when we are humbled by our need, and even when we let others see where we fail, God's amazing goodness and power shine through, changing us and reshaping us from the inside out.

God, I am much weaker than I like to admit or like others to see. Please give me the courage and the integrity to acknowledge my weakness and allow Your power to work in and through me. Thank You that when I am weak, You are strong. Amen.

How do you feel about weakness? Are there ways you try to cover it up or overcome it on your own?

In what area of life do you feel weak right now?

Does knowing God's grace and power show up in our weakness change how you feel about it? Why or why not?

How does support from a community of friends help during times of hardship, persecution, or difficulty? How does that relate to God's promise to be strong in our weakness?

24

COME ALIVE
TO FREEDOM

If you hold to my teaching, you are really my disciples. Then you will know the truth, and the truth will set you free.

—John 8:31–32

The truth will set us free. Does that mean we are captives? Reading Jesus's words, we have to take a step back and realize that if we need to be set free, that means we are prisoners or slaves in need of freedom. But what holds us? Jesus spoke these words to the Jews who had heard Him teach and had believed Him. He went on to tell them that everyone who sins is a slave to sin. That means us—every single one of us is a slave. No matter what we do, we cannot change that identity. We cannot set ourselves free.

But Jesus came to bring freedom. He is the truth. And when we know Him and believe His teachings, we are set free. Our captor is defeated; our identity is changed. We don't just have a little more freedom; we are actually free! As John wrote, "If the Son sets you free, you will be free indeed" (John 8:36). Jesus's work on the cross gives Him the power to grant freedom from death and set free from sin all who believe.

God, thank You for Your sacrifice. Thank You that through Your Son, I am truly free from the thing that holds every one of us captive. Please help me to know Your truth, to hold to Your teachings, and to live the life of freedom that You bring. Amen.

In what ways do you still live like a captive?

How is the freedom Jesus offers similar or different from freedom as our culture understands it?

What step is Christ calling you to take into His freedom?

How will you walk differently today knowing you have been freed from slavery to sin?

25

COME ALIVE
TO ABUNDANCE

The thief comes only to steal and kill and destroy; I have
come that they may have life, and have it to the full.

—John 10:10

Abundant life sounds great, right? But throughout history and still today, Christians disagree about exactly what this means. Is it material prosperity? Then what about the people who sacrificed everything and became poor through serving Christ? Is it peace and comfort? Then what about the faithful who suffered or still suffer for their beliefs? Clearly there is no one pattern for a full life, but God does promise it. So how can we come alive to abundant life when it's so hard to define?

It starts with seeing that God has already given us abundant life. He has taken our sin, which was deserving of death, and replaced it with grace, forgiveness, and open relationship with Himself. Whatever the outside of our life looks like, Jesus is the source of abundant life from within. Abiding with Him fills us to overflowing. Perhaps that is the central part of abundance we often miss. When we overflow with anything—grace, peace, love, hope, gratitude, energy, knowledge, material possessions—that overflow spreads to other people. God's abundance is meant to be shared with others. When we are so full of God, it is Him that the world sees in and through us every day. He fills us with His fullness so that we all may have life.

God, thank You for the abundant gift of Your Son, Jesus. Please help me to open my heart more and more to You so that as I am filled, You will overflow to the world around me. Thank You that You bring life to the full. Amen.

Do you feel like you are living an abundant life in Christ? Why or why not?

What takes that fullness away? How can you open your heart and life to His fullness?

Who does God's abundance overflow to around you?

What does that look like, and how does it bring abundant life to you and others?

26

COME ALIVE
TO GRATITUDE

Give thanks to the LORD, for he is good;
his love endures forever.

—Psalm 107:1

Psychology research consistently shows that gratitude is strongly associated with greater happiness. When we spend time purposefully thinking about the things we are thankful for, it results in a more positive outlook on life. But the writer of this psalm knew that without a scientific study. And not only does gratitude improve our attitude, it also brings us closer in relationship to God. The more we know Him and understand His love for us, the more we recognize and give thanks for His goodness and love.

So how can we come alive to gratitude? Some very practical things can help. Create a journal, and write down five things you are thankful for each day. Spend time in prayer, thanking God for who He is and what He has done. Make a list of people who have helped you in life and the ways God has used them to shape you. Take a walk, and thank God for the amazing things you notice in nature. Being purposeful about giving thanks can help form a habit and allow gratitude to become a cycle that continues to draw us closer to the heart of God.

God, there are so many things to be thankful for. Thank You most of all that You sent Your Son to live, die, and rise again so that we can have Your true, deep, and unending life. Please help me to consistently look for and give thanks for the many gifts You have given. Amen.

What are you thankful for today?

When was the last time you said thank you to God? When do you find it difficult to be thankful?

What are your thoughts about gratitude as a discipline and a habit? How have you seen this develop in your own life or the life of someone you know?

How can sharing with others what you are thankful for help build a spirit of gratitude among friends and family?

27

COME ALIVE
TO YOUR FAMILY

Love is patient, love is kind. It does not envy, it does not boast, it is not proud. It does not dishonor others, it is not self-seeking, it is not easily angered, it keeps no record of wrongs. Love does not delight in evil but rejoices with the truth. It always protects, always trusts, always hopes, always perseveres. Love never fails.

—1 Corinthians 13:4–8

Family. For some, it's the greatest blessing. For others, the greatest curse. But no matter what our family history, those relationships are challenging. Often the people we are closest to are the most difficult to understand, love, and live with. So how can you come alive to your family? It will look different for every person in every stage of life, but the guiding principles of love are the bedrock.

The thirteenth chapter of 1 Corinthians is often referred to as the love chapter because it spells out what love looks like in action. It's no easy road! None of us can love like this in our own strength. But God's love in us can allow us to take steps in each relationship to be more patient, more kind, less proud, less angry. And while the last statement of the verses above ("Love never fails") may seem like an impossible task—and may remind some of us of the pain when human love did fail—it is also a promise. God's perfect love never fails. We can rest in and draw from His love for us and for our families as we work toward more loving relationships.

God, thank You for this description of love and for being the perfect model of love. Please heal the hurt in my family and draw us closer together. Allow Your love to flow through me to all of my family members. Amen.

How would you describe your family relationships?

What makes it challenging to love your family members? What makes it easy?

Based on the 1 Corinthians definition of love, in what ways can you work on loving your family members better?

How can you be family for those who don't have family or have completely lost relationship with them?

28

COME ALIVE
TO YOUR COMMUNITY

Be devoted to one another in love. Honor one another above yourselves. Never be lacking in zeal, but keep your spiritual fervor, serving the Lord. Be joyful in hope, patient in affliction, faithful in prayer. Share with the Lord's people who are in need. Practice hospitality.

—Romans 12:10–13

When you look around your community, do you see strangers or friends? Or maybe you see some of both. The idea of practicing hospitality has a long history in the Bible but comes down to paying attention to the needs of others and helping them feel that they belong. It's about making strangers into guests and guests into friends. It's about building community. It doesn't have to mean gourmet meals and spotlessly clean homes. In fact, those things may be more about the person giving than the person receiving. Instead, hospitality is an openness to share, to honor others, to serve them, and to invite them into relationship.

When we come alive to community, our eyes are opened to the ways in which we can serve those around us. That can be tough—it's why Paul said we must be joyful in hope, patient in affliction, and faithful in prayer. It involves seeing needs, praying for others, reaching out to serve, and welcoming others into your life. It's exactly what God did when He sent His Son to earth—He invited us to be served, loved, and cared for by the God of the universe. Not because we deserved it or had something to offer or were just the kind of people He liked being around. But He served because He was reaching out to us, motivated by His devotion and love for us.

God, thank You for welcoming me, caring for me, and loving me. Please open my eyes to the people in my community who need the same kind of welcome, and give me the strength to build community based on Your grace and love. Amen.

How would you describe your community?

What are some of the needs you see in your church, neighborhood, school, or city?

What gifts or resources has God given you that you might use to practice hospitality and build community?

Who can you partner with in order to strengthen your effort to share God's love and grace?

29

COME ALIVE
TO YOUR WORLD

*Religion that God our Father accepts as pure and faultless
is this: to look after orphans and widows in their distress
and to keep oneself from being polluted by the world.*

—James 1:27

Religion gets a bad rap—unfortunately, it's deserved in many cases, especially when it comes to our ability to grow stale and institutionalized. That has been happening at least since Jesus's days on earth. He called out groups such as the Pharisees for their hypocrisy, and His words were harsh, calling them "whitewashed tombs, which look beautiful on the outside but on the inside are full of the bones of the dead and everything unclean" (Matthew 23:27). Ouch! And the Pharisees were the people in the Jewish culture who appeared to have it all together spiritually. The problem was they had traded the living God for a checklist of behaviors. They were so devoted to their process of trying to earn God's favor that they were blind to God Himself walking among them. Sadly, we're prone to do the same.

But if religion is a set of spiritual practices, God has a different way. Our tendency is to try to exalt ourselves, but as James explained, God's call is to care for the most vulnerable and needy people. It was widows and orphans in his day, those with no family, no opportunities, no rights. Along with many other people, they are still cast aside and marginalized in our culture. When we allow God's love and life to move us toward reaching, caring for, and lifting up the rejects and the outcasts, we live out true expressions of a life that reflects His priorities. Then we are practicing the steps of God's life-giving ways, and we are changed in the process.

God, teach me to think differently than the ways of my culture. Thank You that Your values turn our world upside down. Open my eyes to the needs around me, and fill me with love for the world as I serve You by loving others. Amen.

Where do you see a need you can step toward meeting?

Has God given you a passion for a certain place or people?

Are there people or a group around you who are rejected or outcast? Where can you build a bridge to let someone know they are seen and valued?

What steps can you take to better understand and love the world?

30

COME ALIVE
TO ETERNITY

Before the mountains were born or you brought forth
the whole world, from everlasting to everlasting you are
God. . . . A thousand years in your sight are like a day
that has just gone by, or like a watch in the night.

—Psalm 90:2, 4

Eternity boggles the mind! Everything we know has a beginning and an end, so the idea of everlasting is impossible to wrap our brains around. Perhaps that is the best thing of all. We worship a God who is beyond time and space and beyond our ability to understand, yet He cares for the smallest details of our lives. He does not fit in our boxes. He defies the constraints of our physical world.

Christ's coming at Easter marked a moment in time that changed everything for our world—that moment brought grace and forgiveness and life in place of sin, death, and judgment. It took us one step closer to the fulfillment of God's promise to redeem all things and make our world right again. And the true beauty is that God's story is so much bigger even than that. God's story stretches out over eternity, and He invites us into that mystery. This is not the end of the story—it is only the beginning of an infinite journey of coming alive in Christ.

God, thank You for the season of Easter and a chance to celebrate and learn about the sacrifice You made and the life You offer each of us. May Your grace and love continue to fill me and change me as I live each day for You. Amen.

What helps you wrap your mind around the concept of eternity? What aspects are most difficult to grasp?

Does eternity sound wonderful or overwhelming to you? What has shaped your ideas of eternity and your feelings about it?

How does eternity change your perspective on today?

How can you best continue on your journey of coming alive in Christ?